POEMS HE'LL

NEVER READ

By

Amber Moss

© 2023 by Amber Moss

Also by Amber Moss

Some Kind of Black

To Her

Bucket of Thorns

CONTENTS

To the men who left me broken...

PART I

HEARTBREAKING

It wasn't over for me.

- The Notebook

POEMS HE'LL NEVER READ

Friday 6:29 PM

I love you.

When you left
I didn't think you'd stay gone.

POEMS HE'LL NEVER READ

At 3 AM
my clock whispers your name.

One of the hardest things to do
is to let go of someone
who has already let go of you.

POEMS HE'LL NEVER READ

I can't believe how weak you made me......

Please ~~don't~~ text me.
Please ~~don't~~ text me.
Please ~~don't~~ text me.
Please ~~don't~~ text me.
Please ~~don't~~ text me.
Please ~~don't~~ text me.
Please ~~don't~~ text me.
Please ~~don't~~ text me.
Please ~~don't~~ text me.
Please ~~don't~~ text me.
Please ~~don't~~ text me.
Please ~~don't~~ text me.
Please ~~don't~~ text me.
Please ~~don't~~ text me.
Please ~~don't~~ text me.
Please ~~don't~~ text me.
Please ~~don't~~ text me.
Please ~~don't~~ text me.

POEMS HE'LL NEVER READ

I wonder where your mind goes
when day turns into night.

At night fall
I feel the grief all over again.

POEMS HE'LL NEVER READ

I think in some ways
the truth ended us
way before the lies.

and for a while
my heart forgot where it belonged.

POEMS HE'LL NEVER READ

I starved for your love
while you filled up on mine.

Is it okay to fall for someone
who can't catch you?

POEMS HE'LL NEVER READ

Today I withered out of bed
praying I don't think of you.

Loving you meant losing myself

but what if I don't want to be found?

Even in the arms of someone else
I feel you.

To-do List

1. Get over him.
2. Get over him.
3. Get over him.
4. Get over him.
5. Get over him.

POEMS HE'LL NEVER READ

I wonder how you talk about me
now that I'm gone.

Have you ever felt loneliness in a room full of people?

I ~~don't~~ miss you.

How foolish it is to be secretly still in love with you.

POEMS HE'LL NEVER READ

In a field full of sunflowers
you were still the brightest.

I need lithium.
I need cannabis.
I need whiskey.
I need amethyst.

I need you.

I only pulled back because I wanted you
to push harder.

Why did you believe me when I said I needed space?

Pieces of me still fall to the ground
without you.

I stained the page of the letter
you wrote me

Forgive me.

POEMS HE'LL NEVER READ

I used to be good at goodbyes

now my tongue won't spell the word.

Do you ever wonder if you were okay before you met them?

Were you whole?

POEMS HE'LL NEVER READ

Wed, Sep 13 at 5:56 PM

You are gorgeous babe

Please don't look at someone else
the way you looked at me.

How dare you go back to being a stranger?

I should've saved myself before I met you
if you weren't going to be the hero.

POEMS HE'LL NEVER READ

For a moment there
I thought you'd fight for me.

The problem with holding onto hope
is how easily it can slip away.

POEMS HE'LL NEVER READ

Give me a new brain
this one holds too many memories.

I'd rather have every argument again
than the silence invading my bedroom.

Please ~~don't~~ call me.
Please ~~don't~~ call me.
Please ~~don't~~ call me.
Please ~~don't~~ call me.
Please ~~don't~~ call me.
Please ~~don't~~ call me.
Please ~~don't~~ call me.
Please ~~don't~~ call me.
Please ~~don't~~ call me.
Please ~~don't~~ call me.
Please ~~don't~~ call me.
Please ~~don't~~ call me.
Please ~~don't~~ call me.
Please ~~don't~~ call me.
Please ~~don't~~ call me.
Please ~~don't~~ call me.
Please ~~don't~~ call me.
Please ~~don't~~ call me.

I heard your name in the grocery store
but I couldn't turn my head.

I prayed for the first time in months
to finally be able to forget you.

I hate that my duvet still smells like you.

I convinced myself that loving you would never hurt.

I loved you at your worst
yet,
you couldn't love me at my best.

Most math problems are solvable.

Too bad we're not an equation.

Fri, Feb 13 at 10:53 AM

I'm not worried about a lot of women
I was only worried about you.

My dream house still has pictures of you on the walls.

and sometimes I wear your plain t-shirt
just for comfort.

The darkness isn't all bad. I trace your face
in the stars and watch for airplanes
wondering if you're in one.

This is my new peace.

Time is moving so slowly without you. Time is
moving so slowly without you. Time is moving
so slowly without you. Time   is   moving   so
s l o w l y

       without

                      you.

You're still my favorite person.

and at the end of it all
I just hope I made you a better person.

PART II

HEALING.

Your tears are a reminder that you knew love.

Don't ignore the lump in your throat.

You're allowed to let it out.

Whenever you start to miss him
count to 10.

POEMS HE'LL NEVER READ

1. 2. 3. 4. 5. 6. 7. 8. 9. 10.

How many times did you tell him you love him
and he didn't feel it back?

What's amazing is
you still have so much to offer someone else.

What if your insecurities are only visible to you?

What if you find all the love you need
within yourself?

There is beauty in a bandaged heart.

When you let go of what was, to find what's new,
I promise you'll smile again.

ABOUT THE AUTHOR

Amber Moss is a poet in Atlanta. She graduated from the University of South Florida with a Bachelor's degree in English. She is the author of two full-length poetry collections and two chapbooks. Her latest chapbook, Some Kind of Black was released in February 2022 (Nymeria Publishing). She completed a writer's residency at Sundress Academy for the Arts. Her individual poems have been published in Alan Squire Publishing, Little Rose Magazine, Liminality Magazine, Poetry Super Highway, and others.